DOGS SET X

ROTTWEILERS

Tamara L. Britton
ABDO Publishing Company

visit us at
www.abdopublishing.com

Published by ABDO Publishing Company, PO Box 398166, Minneapolis, MN 55439.
Copyright © 2013 by Abdo Consulting Group, Inc. International copyrights reserved
in all countries. No part of this book may be reproduced in any form without written
permission from the publisher. The Checkerboard Library™ is a trademark and logo of
ABDO Publishing Company.

Printed in the United States of America, North Mankato, Minnesota.
102012
012013

Cover Photo: Alamy
Interior Photos: Alamy p. 19; AP Images p. 7; Corbis pp. 5, 8, 13;
        iStockphoto pp. 10–11, 15, 16–17, 21; Thinkstock pp. 9, 16, 18

Editors: Megan M. Gunderson, Stephanie Hedlund
Art Direction: Neil Klinepier

Cataloging-in-Publication Data

Britton, Tamara L., 1963-
 Rottweilers / Tamara L. Britton.
    p. cm. -- (Dogs)
 Includes bibliographical references and index.
 ISBN 978-1-61783-591-9
 1. Rottweiler dog--Juvenile literature. 2. Dogs--Juvenile literature. I. Title.
636.73--dc23
                        2012946331

CONTENTS

THE DOG FAMILY

Dogs come in many shapes and sizes. Yet, all of these dogs belong to the family **Canidae**. The name comes from the Latin word for "dog," which is *canis*.

For more than 12,000 years, dogs and humans have lived and worked together. Early humans adopted wolf pups and trained them to be hunting dogs. These wolves are the ancestors of modern dogs.

Over time, humans began **breeding** dogs for other activities. They have developed more than 400 dog breeds. These breeds fill many different roles. Rottweilers are working dogs. They were bred to guard and herd animals.

The Rottweiler

ROTTWEILERS

Historians believe that the Rottweiler is the descendant of herding dogs. In AD 74, these dogs accompanied Roman soldiers into what would become Rottweil in southern Germany. Their job was to herd and guard the livestock that the soldiers kept for food.

During the Middle Ages, the dogs became service dogs. Many local butchers owned a Rottweiler. The Rottweiler carried its owner's money in a pack around its neck.

By the 1800s, the number of Rottweilers had declined. To preserve the **breed**, German admirers formed a club in 1901. Club members created a breed standard for the dogs. Slowly, the Rottweiler's popularity increased.

This male Rottweiler named Pilot won the best of breed award at the 2012 Westminster Kennel Club Dog Show.

In 1931, Rottweilers were recognized by the **American Kennel Club**. In 1973, the American Rottweiler Club was established. Today, the Rottweiler is the tenth most popular **breed** in the United States.

WHAT THEY'RE LIKE

Rottweilers are working dogs. So, they are happiest when they have a job to do. These intelligent dogs excel at police work, service work, and ranch work.

Rottweilers love to show off and please their owners. They often follow their owners around the house so they can be near them.

Rottweilers are friendly toward

Rottweilers can be hard to handle if not properly trained.

their family and friends. But, they are protective of their people and their territory. They do not welcome strangers. Rottweilers can be **aggressive**. Obedience training and **socialization** are a must for these devoted animals.

But a well-trained Rottweiler can be a loving pet!

COAT AND COLOR

Rottweilers have a double coat. The straight, medium-length outer coat is rough and **dense**. Shorter hair covers the Rottweiler's head, ears, and legs. The coat is longest on the **breeches**.

The outer coat is black. It has mahogany, rust, or tan markings. The markings are on the dog's face, **muzzle**, throat, and legs, and the area under its tail.

The undercoat is gray, tan, or black. It is located on the dog's neck and thighs. But you can't see it through the outer coat! The undercoat can be thick or thin, depending on the climate where the dog lives.

Ninety percent of a Rottweiler's coat is black.

SIZE

Rottweilers are medium to large dogs. They are longer than they are tall. Males stand 24 to 27 inches (61 to 69 cm) at the shoulders. Females are 22 to 25 inches (56 to 64 cm) tall.

The Rottweiler is a sturdy dog. Strong, straight legs support its well-muscled body and deep chest. The tail is **cropped**. An excited Rottweiler will carry its tail up!

The Rottweiler's **muzzle** is broad at the face and tapers to a black nose. Its ears are set far apart on the head and hang forward. Its dark brown, almond-shaped eyes are set deep. These features give the Rottweiler its powerful look.

A female Rottweiler *(right)* is slightly smaller than a male.

CARE

Daily exercise will help keep your Rottweiler mentally and physically fit. Regular grooming is also important. And, grooming time gives you an opportunity to check your dog's feet, ears, and eyes for problems.

Rottweilers **shed** quite a bit. Regular brushing can help manage all that fur! Rottweilers need their nails clipped regularly, too.

Like all dogs, Rottweilers need veterinary care. A veterinarian can give them **vaccines**. He or she can also **spay** or **neuter** puppies.

Though robust, Rottweilers can have some health problems. Joint, eye, and heart problems are common in this **breed**. Your veterinarian can watch for these issues.

Brushing your Rottie's teeth every day with toothpaste made just for dogs will help keep your dog healthy.

FEEDING

Rottweilers are active dogs that need a well-balanced diet. A high-quality commercial dog food will provide the proper **nutrients**. Rottweilers must be exercised every day so they do not gain weight.

When you buy a puppy, continue with the same food it was eating at the **breeder**'s. A

It is easy to be talked into extra food by a charming Rottie!

16

small puppy needs about three meals a day. It will need just two by the time it is six months old. An adult dog can eat just once a day.

Don't let your Rottweiler go thirsty! A constant supply of fresh water is especially important for this large **breed**.

But an overweight dog is not healthy or happy.

THINGS THEY NEED

A large, fenced yard will keep your Rottweiler safe. It will also offer some freedom of movement. But don't leave these active animals alone. They are people dogs. They will react poorly to being alone for extended periods.

Your Rottie's bed will be a safe haven. It will learn to go there for a break!

Playing with toys will give your Rottie the mental and physical stimulation it needs.

After a busy day, your Rottweiler will need a quiet place to rest. A crate or a soft bed is the perfect spot for a dog to relax.

You will need to provide a few other items for your dog. These include a leash, a collar, and license and identification tags. Sturdy food and water bowls are a must. And don't forget the treats!

PUPPIES

Like all dogs, a mother Rottweiler is **pregnant** for about 63 days. She will give birth to 6 to 10 puppies. The newborn puppies are completely dependent on their mother. They begin to see and hear after about 10 to 14 days.

After three weeks, the young Rottweilers will begin exploring their surroundings. When they are 14 to 16 weeks old, they are ready for adoption.

Is a Rottweiler the right dog for you? If so, look for a reputable **breeder**. Start training your new puppy right away. This will help it grow into a well-adjusted dog.

Over time, introduce your puppy to new people and surroundings. Allowing the dog to make friends will make it a happier pet. Rottweilers make loyal family members for about 10 years.

In some countries, such as England, it is against the law to crop a pet Rottweiler's tail.

GLOSSARY

aggressive (uh-GREH-sihv) - displaying hostility.

American Kennel Club - an organization that studies and promotes interest in purebred dogs.

breeches - longer fur on a dog's thighs.

breed - a group of animals sharing the same ancestors and appearance. A breeder is a person who raises animals. Raising animals is often called breeding them.

Canidae (KAN-uh-dee) - the scientific Latin name for the dog family. Members of this family are called canids. They include wolves, jackals, foxes, coyotes, and domestic dogs.

crop - to cut off the upper or outer part of something.

dense - thick or compact.

muzzle - an animal's nose and jaws.

neuter (NOO-tuhr) - to remove a male animal's reproductive glands.

nutrient - a substance found in food and used in the body. It promotes growth, maintenance, and repair.

pregnant - having one or more babies growing within the body.

shed - to cast off hair, feathers, skin, or other coverings or parts by a natural process.

socialize - to adapt an animal to behaving properly around people or other animals in various settings.

spay - to remove a female animal's reproductive organs.

vaccine (vak-SEEN) - a shot given to prevent illness or disease.

WEB SITES

To learn more about Rottweilers, visit ABDO Publishing Company online. Web sites about Rottweilers are featured on our Book Links page. These links are routinely monitored and updated to provide the most current information available.

www.abdopublishing.com

INDEX